G.L. OTTO

HOUSE OF DEBT

The Ultimate Guide on How to Manage Your Debt, Discover Effective Debt Consolidation Strategies So You Can Eliminate Your Debt Once and For All

Descrierea CIP a Bibliotecii Naționale a României
G.L. OTTO
    HOUSE OF DEBT. The Ultimate Guide on How to Manage Your Debt, Discover Effective Debt Consolidation Strategies So You Can Eliminate Your Debt Once and For All / G.L. Otto –
Bucharest: Editura My Ebook, 2021
    ISBN

G.L. OTTO

HOUSE OF DEBT

The Ultimate Guide on How to Manage Your Debt, Discover Effective Debt Consolidation Strategies So You Can Eliminate Your Debt Once and For All

My Ebook Publishing House
Bucharest, 2021

TABLE OF CONTENTS

Foreword 7

Chapter 1: *Introduction* 9
Chapter 2: *Debt consolidation* 11
Chapter 3: *Strategies Of Debt Consolidation* 17
Chapter 4: *How To Be A Good Debt Manager* 21
Chapter 5: *Factors To Be Considered In Debt Consolidation* 25
Chapter 6: *Re-Financing to Consolidate Debt* 29
Chapter 7: *Student Loan Consolidation* 33
Chapter 8: *Ways To Save Money* 37

Wrapping Up: *More Ways To Boost Your Consolidation Skills* 41

FOREWORD

Falling into the trap of unmanageable debt is a very common situation nowadays. It is a proven fact that more than 40% of US people spends more than what they earn and very obviously most of them experience the difficulty of paying debt at the right time. Get all the info you need here.

Debt Consolidation Strategies
How To Become Great At Managing Debt

CHAPTER 1

INTRODUCTION

Synopsis

Climbing out of the trap of debt could be a real complicated process without using any proper procedure. Are you also one of them and swimming in the financial hot water? Do you really know any solution?

The Basics

Well debt consolidation plan is the real savior which can actually bring you out of the situation. Debt consolidation helps you to pay off/clear your multiple loans at a same time. It is done with an objective of securing a fixed interest rate or lesser interest rate.

Now you might be eager to know the complete details about debt consolidation. Well, here I am going to discuss the entire details about it.

CHAPTER 2

DEBT CONSOLIDATION

Synopsis

Here I am going to tell you all about debt consolidation so that you will get a clear idea about the entire process of debt consolidation.

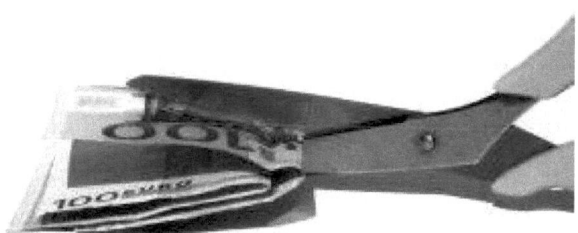

What Is Debt Consolidation

Generally, you can find there are two types of debts but each of them has different sub types included. Loans are one.

Loans are offered for fixed amounts and are not reusable after paying it off. You can have several types of loans and the following are the loan types.

Personal Loan - This type of loan is offered for a specific amount of money. A personal loan is given for a declared and undeclared usage. This type of loan is processed through a bank or other authentic financial lending institute. Secured loans are given to anyone against property or guarantor but unsecured loans are only provided to the consumers with a high credit rating.

Mortgage Loan - It is a long term loan and mortgage loans are specifically issued for purchasing personal or commercial property. As a customer, here you might negotiate to lower the monthly payment.

Educational Loan - This type of loan is particularly designed for educational purpose only. Educational loans are issued for paying educational bills, hostel fees, tuition fees and other living expenses for college or university. This type of loan is paid after completing the course successfully. In this type of loan you can ask for an additional grace period.

Now these are the typical traditional loans and the second type of debt is revolving credit. It is really important to know what revolving credit is. Unlike traditional loans, it allows you to borrow the same amount of money again after paying the loan amount.

There are mainly two types of revolving credit you can find in the market and they are-

- Credit Card
- Line of Credit

Credit Card

Yes today we all use plastic money. I am sure that you are aware of the fact that a credit card is called plastic money. Today a credit card has become the most common form of personal debt. According to the latest surveys, it is said that almost each American has more than five credit cards on average.

Line of Credit

Generally, a line of credit is issued by banks and other financial organizations. It provides a reusable source of funds and you can withdraw it by check or cash.

So now you have probably have a good idea about different forms of debts but we are not going to talk about debt but debt consolidation.

Now the question might come up… why I told you so many things about debt when the main topic is debt consolidation here.

Well, the reason is very simple; without knowing what debt is you would not be able to understand what debt consolidation is.

Today everything seems alright in your financial world and you are happy and completely free of worry but tomorrow could be the day when you might have to face a very hectic situation. No one knows about tomorrow.

There are many situations where people find themselves unable to pay off the current debt obligation. Due to the recent financial crisis, a lot of people have lost their job and for them, paying the debt is just impossible. What if you are also one of them? Have you ever thought about it?

The devaluation of many homes, properties, resulting in negative equity, is one of the most crucial reasons why most people are still unable to get rid of the burden of debt. Especially after the last housing bubble burst, most of the US homes have lost 28% of their value on an average.

One of the most practical ways to pay off the insurmountable debt is nothing but debt consolidation.

Usually there are two types of debt consolidation but it comes in one of two forms- Home Equity Loan and Negotiated Debt Settlement

Home Equity Loan

This is one of the most effective debt consolidation solutions for mortgage customers. This type of debt consolidation loan allows a customer to refinance their mortgage. Here the customer can use the equity amount that he built up as a loan guarantee. Here the consumer can use the same amount to pay off the higher interest loans and credit card loans.

With the help of this home equity loan, home owners just have to pay one single payment per month which is definitely lesser than the total combined monthly loan amount of all the outstanding loans.

Negotiated Debt Settlement

This is another type of debt consolidation loan. It includes the involvement of a third party service which is specialized in debt consolidation.

It is very obvious that you want to know about the exact services you will get. Usually the third party will contact each of the creditors personally on behalf of you. Here the third party service will negotiate an amount and you have to pay that amount every month. The advantage of going for this sort of settlement is that the negotiated amount will be always lesser than actual loan amount.

All you have to do is pay the money to the third party and they will make the payment to each of the creditors.

Just like any other financial planning, debt consolidation also requires some smart strategies to follow. The more effective your debt consolidation strategy is, the more easily you will be able to get rid of the debt. Now it is really important to follow some effective strategies and here I am going to discuss some highly effective debt consolidation strategies with you.

CHAPTER 3

STRATEGIES OF DEBT CONSOLIDATION

Synopsis

If you are just like many other people and find yourself trapped into the debt crisis, then you are at the ideal place. All is not lost! Rather there are different ways in which you can turn the situation around. My main purpose is to give you some insight into the crucial things that you should do and the options that you have.

There are number of strategies to tackle the situation very easily and here I am going to describe the strategies that you need to follow.

Strategies

Make a Budget

Making a proper budget is the most important thing that you should do. Do you know what the purpose of making budget is? A budget will help you to track the incoming and outgoing money.

A well developed budget always helps people to make a plan so that they can live below their means instead of living beyond it. Yes, it helps to change the entire mindset about money so that people can save more money and the more money you will save the sooner you will be able to pay off the debt completely.

Budget making is the most important debt consolidation strategy that you can implement.

Sell some assets in order to pay your debts

I am sure that you know about E Bay. Do you know how much money E Bay makes each year? Billions! If you have excess amount of assets then you could easily sell some of them to get those debts under control.

Pay more on debts on a monthly basis

If you pay more than the minimum amount then you will be able to get rid of all the debts sooner and easily.

Try to do the same thing with all of your debts that you can afford. It would be better if you do this than with a loan with the higher interest rate.

Restructure your mortgage payment

If you want to reduce the mortgage loan payment amount in a significant way then you should implement a bi-weekly mortgage system. It will help you to reduce the rate of interest significantly.

It will surely help you to pay off the loan amount completely.

Refinancing

If you have your own house and want to obtain a lower interest rate then a refinance could be the best option.

But if you are unable to get a lower interest rate for your mortgage loan or there will be a penalty then you can go for equity loan or line of credit.

A loan secured by other personal property

If you have any expensive car or boat then you can easily get a loan against that and you can use the same loan amount to pay off other debts.

An unsecured loan

Unsecured loans are the only option if you do not have any other loan options.

CHAPTER 4

HOW TO BE A GOOD DEBT MANAGER

Synopsis

There's nothing more we want than to be able to efficiently manage our cash. After all, the cash that we wish to manage is cash that's frequently, hard earned. This is where a budget comes in. A budget executed the right way, ought to help you see where your cash is going, get more utility out of every dollar, and help you save some extra for future use.

How To

The 1st smart secret to a budget is to set a goal. What do you wish to accomplish? Do you want to correctly appropriate your revenue into bill payments? Do you wish to put an amount aside for a huge purchase or a large investment? By having a goal, you'll be able to shape your budget to best serve your interests.

Secondly, you'd want to take note of where your cash commonly goes. This includes bills, major but regular purchases (like market costs, healthcare costs, and the like), and daily miscellaneous purchases.

Only when you list where you know your cash commonly goes will you be able to distinguish which expenses you may do without. Once you've identified these regular expenditures, take into consideration what you may cut down on.

How much do you spend on your every day caffeine fix in the morning? How much do you spend on paper deliveries to your front door? The paltry $2 or $5 of these little purchases cumulatively translates to more than $3600 a year!

Rather than buying your expensive latte or reading the paper in print, put aside the amount you'd commonly pay for these little routine purchases in a little container. You'll be surprised at how much you're saving out of your old budget.

Being indebted is a vicious cycle on its own. You're talking about continuous payments, let alone large interest rates. The best way to deal with this is to pay the lower limit on all of your debts in order to avoid paying extraneous late fees.

Whatever money excesses you may have, you may opt to add on to the payments you make in your greatest debt. This way, you're centered on getting the greatest debts first that cost you the greatest interest rates. Doing this more and more, you'll be amazed at how much you'll take off your large debts.

The last and most crucial step is to jot down the amount you earn the sum you spend. You may make use of computer cash management programs, or make database sheets of your own. Make a system that works for you and will help you keep track of your monthly budgeting progression.

CHAPTER 5

FACTORS TO BE CONSIDERED IN DEBT CONSOLIDATION

Synopsis

Is consolidating charge card debt a good option?

Well, the answer will more often be yes than no. Consolidating charge card debt is frequently regarded as the opening move towards charge card debt elimination. All the same, even before you move to take first step toward consolidating charge card debt, you have to understand that consolidating charge card debt (or balance transfer) is an action that you're taking to eliminate charge card debt. Consolidating charge card debt isn't a means of deferring the issue for later.

Consolidating

Consolidating charge card debt is indeed a great option in more than one sense. Not only do you get relief from the speedy increase in your charge card debt, but likewise get additional advantages too. Offers for consolidating charge card debt are in abundance and are really attractive indeed.

Almost all the offers for consolidating charge card debt have an initial low APR period during which the APR is commonly 0% (or some low figure). As a matter of fact, this is one of the main things which make consolidating charge card debt a really attractive option.

Besides this low APR, the offers for consolidating charge card debt likewise include things like no interest rate on the purchases made during first five months (or some other initial period) of balance transfer. This is another thing that lowers the speed at which your charge card debt extends.

So these are the two most important advantages that charge card suppliers deploy to attract individuals into consolidating charge card debt with them. Then there are additional advantages which include things like additional reward points on the member's reward program of the charge card you're consolidating charge card debt to.

These reward points may be redeemed for other attractive goods/rebates/rewards etc. Occasionally, the new charge card (i.e. the one you're consolidating charge card debt to) may be a charge card that caters more to your present spending needs both in terms of the charge limits and the way you spend your cash.

For instance, the new charge card could be a co-branded one offered by an airline that you've started travelling with very frequently and consolidating charge card debt on such a card might be much more advantages as compared to your current charge card which was based on your needs at the time. The charge card you're consolidating charge card debt with may open up discount offers to you.

CHAPTER 6

RE-FINANCING TO CONSOLIDATE DEBT

Synopsis

A few homeowners opt to re-finance to consolidate their existing debts. With this sort of option, the homeowner may consolidate higher interest debts like charge card debts under a lower interest home loan. The interest rates affiliated with home loans are traditionally lower than the rates affiliated with charge cards by a considerable amount.

Deciding whether or not to re-finance for the purpose of debt consolidation may be a kind of tricky issue. There are a number of complex elements which enter into the equation including the total of existing debt, the difference in interest rates as well as the difference in loan terms and the present financial state of the homeowner.

Refinancing

The term debt consolidation may be fairly confusing as the term itself is fairly deceptive. When a homeowner re-finances his home for the purpose of debt consolidation, he is not really consolidating the debt in the true sense of the word. By definition to consolidate means to combine or to merge into one system. But, this isn't what really occurs when debts are consolidated. The existing debts are really repaid by the debt consolidation loan. Although the total sum of debt stays constant, the individual debts are repaid by the new loan.

Before the debt consolidation the homeowner might have been repaying a monthly debt to one or more charge card companies, a car lender, a student loan lender or any number of additional lenders but now the homeowner is repaying one debt to the mortgage lender who supplied the debt consolidation loan. This fresh loan will be subject to the applicable loan terms including rates of interest and repayment period. Any terms affiliated with the individual loans are no longer valid, as each of these loans has been paid back in full.

When thinking about debt consolidation it's crucial to determine whether lower monthly payments or an overall increase in savings is being sought. This is a crucial consideration as while debt consolidation may lead to lower monthly payments if a lower interest mortgage is obtained to repay higher interest debts there is not always a total cost savings. This is because interest rate alone doesn't determine the amount which will be paid in interest. The total of debt and the loan term, or length of the loan, figure prominently into the equation too.

As an illustration, consider a debt with a comparatively short loan term of 5 years and an interest only somewhat higher than the rate associated with the debt consolidation loan. In that case, if the term of the debt consolidation loan were 30 years the repayment of the original loan would be extended over the course of 30 years at a rate of interest which is only somewhat lower than the original rate. In that case, it's clear the homeowner could end up paying more in the long run. But, the monthly payments will likely be drastically reduced. This sort of decision forces the homeowner to decide whether a total savings or lower monthly payments is more crucial.

Homeowners who are thinking about re-financing for the purpose of debt consolidation ought to carefully consider whether or not their financial situation will be bettered by re-financing. This is crucial as some homeowners might opt to re-finance as it increases their monthly cash flow even if it doesn't result in a total cost savings. There are a lot of mortgage calculators available on the Net which may be used for purposes like determining whether or not monthly cash flow will increase. Utilizing these calculators and consulting with industry experts will help the homeowner to make an intelligent decision.

CHAPTER 7

STUDENT LOAN CONSOLIDATION

Synopsis

Student loan consolidation has much to offer. That's what a lot of experts often say. To discover what consolidation has to offer, let's read on.

Student Loans

Over time, the student loans you've borrowed have been specified with assorted variable interest rates. Note that the key word here is variable. While the loan you got might have offered, say, 3.5 percent initially, the rate will actually go up as the rates of interest go up. So, if you have 2 or more of these loans, there's a great chance that you might have owed amounts at assorted rates, and these rates may rise and fall yearly.

Considering that, the interest rates have nowhere else to go but up, it's no doubt a safe bet that the debt you have accrued will mount faster than it would if you think about a student loan consolidation.

By thinking about consolidation and remaining on your ten years payment plan, it's possible that you are able to lock your interest at today's current loan rates and save a few bucks over the long run. Apart from that, all of those loans that might have come from different lending companies or banks may be a burden to deal with.

So, if you consolidate, it means that you simply deal with one exclusive company and one payment instead of several. Other than that, you have the amazing chance to get added bonuses like payment and interest rate decreases in case you pay your debts on time over a period of months. These advantages are likewise possible to come if you have automatically withdrawn your monthly payment from a checking or savings account.

In the government consolidation loan programs, it's interesting to realize that there are really no deadlines connected to it. It is supported by the fact that you may apply for the student loan anytime during the grace period or even on the repayment period. However to consolidate student loans, a few considerations must be paid attention.

To consolidate student loans, you ought to realize that it commonly take place during your grace period. At this time, the lower in-school interest rate will then be applied to approximate the weighted average fixed rate to consolidate student loans. And once the grace period has finished on your government student loans, the higher in-repayment rate of interest will be applied to approximate the weighted average fixed rate. Given such process, it's then understandable that your fixed interest rate for government student loan consolidation will be bigger if you consolidate student loans after your grace period.

And when you're interested in consolidating student loans, you ought to understand that even of your student loans are already in repayment, consolidating student loans is still allowed and advantageous. It's for the reason that when you consolidate student loans at this time, you already fix the interest rate on your government student loans while the rates are still low.

CHAPTER 8

WAYS TO SAVE MONEY

Synopsis

The word "frugality" has left a more negative connotation for most individuals than merely being a saver, a tightwad or cheapskate. There's a thin line difference to saving and too much frugality to the point of being awkward and absurd. This is where the negative connotation comes from.

But if you're guided with the correct principles and reasons in deciding to live a frugal life, you will never go wrong.

If you've decided to live frugally, no need to be worried about insults. Keep your head up high. And keep your focus on these tips.

Tips

1. *Dining out* - Having meet ups with friends on a Friday night is all right if you do it once in a while. However, this can be expensive if you add them up at the end of the month.

2. *Clothing* - of course, if you're the kind of individual who loves signature and designer clothes, don't expect that there will be something left from your take home pay. Rather than being trendy, wear clothes that may easily be matched with your other clothes.

3. *Owning a Home* - If you're planning to move out and find a place to settle, don't get overwhelmed by the excitement, rather be practical. As a start, purchase a smaller house or try

other ways like rent-to-own, do-it-yourself arrangements, and owner financing.

4. *Purchasing Your Own automobile* - Shy away from sports cars or SUVs. Simply stick to your purpose of purchasing an automobile which is to transport you where you need to go. Check into also things like a new automobile warranty. Perhaps this isn't the best time to replace your automobile with a new one.

5. *Shopping for Groceries* - As much as possible don't go with items that are brand names. Search for off-brands and try looking for items on the highest or lowest shelves for best prices. Grab the opportunity and shop during sales or use coupons.

6. *Family Out* - There are cheap ways to bond with your loved ones and be entertained like going to libraries, local parks, picnics, visit friends and local church.

7. *Purchasing School Supplies* - Stock school supplies at home and don't purchase anything fancy.

8. *Be content with what you have and try to live within what you earn.*

9. *Plan your Child's College Education* - Teach them the ways to be independent and self-supporting by encouraging them to apply for scholarships and "on campus jobs".

10. Be Aware of your financial limits

11. *Anticipate your failures by Planning* - Have always a budget plan so you will avoid impulsive purchasing.

Wrapping Up

More Ways To Boost Your Consolidation Skills

With a debt consolidation plan consumers are able to get rid of debts quickly and conveniently. Although this loan does not pay off all debts at one go, it surely takes care of them in a more systematic manner.

A person is no longer required to make innumerable calculations for paying off monthly debts (from loans and credit cards). Each and every month needn't be a month of low finances and heavy interest payments. A good consolidation plan immensely assists in managing all financial debts responsibly and wisely.

Go for popular and authentic professional consolidation

In the market there are innumerable debt consolidation plans, each aiming towards reducing financial pressure for the consumer. When such professional help is used, one can easily shift the payment stress from oneself on to the consolidation plan.

This single loan will handle all the personal loans, car loans, student loans and credit card loans. In-return the consumer is required to pay a single debt which is lower in interest.

There is only one payment to be calculated, only one date to be remembered and only one payment to be made every month. This is a gift in disguise as it gives the consumer a break from the financial stress.

However, it is highly important to get a debt consolidation plan which fits otherwise a consumer may suffer monetarily. It is important to check the success records of the consolidation plan. Online reviews of consumers and personal experiences of family and friends are a great help while deciding on a good consolidation plan.

Making yourself aware about credit management methods Getting into an appropriate debt consolidation plan will benefit the consumer in a big way but a bad consolidation plan will lead to total disaster. It is very essential to gain good knowledge about what a debt consolidation plan has to offer. Reading articles written by previous consumers and financial experts will surely improve consumer's debt consolidation management skills.

Going for debt counseling

Many consumers like to go for a professional consultation before debt consolidation. As a consumer you may not be so sure about the guidelines of a good debt consolidation plan, so professional advice helps in a major way.

There are several consultants who are known to give beneficial advice which can improve the credit health of a consumer. Improved credit would automatically generate larger finances helping people consolidate their credit in a very wise manner.

Successful debt consolidation plans are initiated by consumers who are not obsessed with their finances. On the contrary, they are the relaxed and knowledgeable consumers who are looking towards a long term improvement of credit.

Printed by Libri Plureos GmbH in Hamburg, Germany